Vickie Phelps

Water From God
For Those Thirsty for God's Word

By Vickie Phelps

Contents

Water Stories

When creation of the earth and the seas began, the Spirit of God hovered above the waters (Genesis 1:2). God began the process of dividing the dry land from the waters and filling those bodies of water with life. The humans, animals, plant life, trees, and water creatures needed life-giving water. Without water, they all would wither away and die.

Water is so important to the human body. Every cell and organ in our body needs water to function properly. Dehydration can be fatal. We must stay hydrated so our body can do for us the things we need to carry on daily activities. Even more important is our need for spiritual water. Without the living water that Jesus supplies we cannot obtain eternal life.

The Bible is full of great stories of people God wanted to use, bless, or encourage in one way or another. Water played a part in all these stories in some way. From Moses, a man God used to deliver

His people from Egyptian bondage to Nahum, an important military officer God wanted to heal of leprosy, to the impulsive Peter who stepped out of a boat to walk on water, we learn how God used water as an instrument to bring about victory, defeat, refreshment, and deliverance. We read about water poured out as a sacrifice to God, and water drawn by a bride-to-be when a servant brought her a proposal from his master. These stories teach us life lessons and share truth from God's Word. They illustrate the magnificence and power of God. These stories should encourage us to allow God to use us in His work whatever that may be. All of the scriptures are taken from the New International Version of the Bible.

God: Creation and Water

Today's Reading: Genesis 1:1-31

"In the beginning God created the heavens and the earth. Now the earth was formless and empty, darkness was over the surface of the deep, and the Spirit of God was hovering over the waters" Genesis 1:1-2.

Only the Spirit of God can create something out of nothing. The earth was void and without form, but God's Spirit was present to create. When you consider water, its many uses, and the fact that God commands and controls it, your only conclusion can be that God is the Creator of the universe we live in. In his commentary, Matthew Henry writes, *"The Spirit of God was the first mover: He moved upon the face of the waters."*[1] From there, He began to separate the water and give it

[1] *Genesis - Matthew Henry's Commentary* - Bible Gateway

boundaries. He called the dry land ground and called the gathered waters seas. It was only the beginning of God's use of water.

When you consider the rivers and lakes full of underwater life of all kinds and the way God sends rain to water the earth and gives us water to drink, His works are amazing. He planned everything perfectly. He created our bodies to operate on water. Without it, we will die. As a general rule of thumb, a person can survive without water for about three days. Without water, the body is unable to function correctly, and organs will begin to stop performing their designated job. Every cell in our body requires water.[2] Our body is a miraculous machine, created by God to operate on water.

When we consider all He has made and how much water figures into creation and the universe as a whole, how can we not raise our hearts and voices in praise to the God who created it. In her book, *"Amen and Good Night God,"* author Jo Huddleston says it this way. *"God, You outdid yourself today! Thank you for the much-needed rain you blessed us with."* [3]

And the psalmist wrote it this way.

"Mightier than the thunder of the great waters, mightier than the breakers of the sea— the LORD on high is mighty" Psalm 93:4.

Prayer: God, I praise You for all You have

---

[2] How long can you live without water? Facts and effects (medicalnewstoday.com)

[3] *Amen and Good Night God*, Jo Huddleston, Tyndale House Publishers, Inc., ©1995.

created. Your works are awesome and majestic. You are a creative, loving God, worthy of all praise. Amen.

Vickie Phelps

Moses: Drawn Out of the Water

Today's Reading: Exodus 2:1-10.

"When the child grew older, she took him to
Pharaoh's daughter, and he became her son.
She named him Moses, saying, "I drew him out
of the water" Exodus 2:10.

As a young married woman, I went
fishing with my husband. We didn't
have an expensive boat with a powerful
motor. We had a little aluminum boat that
seemed even smaller when we were in the
middle of the lake. One day I realized just how
vulnerable we were in that tiny craft when a
storm arose, and we were miles from shore. Our
little boat rocked and weaved about on the water
as the wind rose and the sky turned dark. We
could easily have been swept away by the wind
and waves, but we managed to get out of the
water without damage. So did Moses.

Although he was too young to know what was happening to him, he was in the Nile River in a small floating boat all alone. Pharoah had ordered that all male Hebrew babies be destroyed. The Hebrew population had grown tremendously, and the Egyptians were concerned the Hebrews would join up with their enemies and leave them without slaves to serve them. Moses' mother had other thoughts about the Pharoah's order and did what she could to save her son. She crafted a tiny ark out of bulrushes, pitch, and slime then placed Moses inside and set it in the Nile River. He could have been swept downstream or drowned, but God made a way out for him.

Pharoah's daughter came to the river with her maidens to bathe, and while there, she discovered the baby Moses in his tiny floating bed. She recognized him as a Hebrew baby and gave him the name Moses, an anglicized version of the Hebrew name *Moshe* which means to draw or pull out of the water. He grew up in Pharoah's palace with the best of everything, but one day he committed murder and had to run for his life. He ended up in a desert tending sheep, but it wasn't the end for him. It was only the beginning of God's plan for Moses' life. Alone in that desert, God began talking to Moses and called him back to Egypt where he became the leader of the Hebrew people and led them out of bondage and started them on their journey to the promised land.

Do you sometimes feel you are in the

middle of a river in a small boat with no destination in mind? Life is tossing your craft around and sometimes you wonder if you're going to make it. Just like Moses, God has a plan for you. It does not matter where you come from or what you have done in the past. Remember, Moses was a murderer at one point, but God changed him and used him for His purpose. Let God draw you out of the water, change you and use you. He is a merciful God, and those mercies are new every morning.

Prayer: God, when life has me feeling like I'm floating in a small boat without direction show me your plan for my life. Draw me out of the water and use me for your glory. Amen.

Marah: Water Fit to Drink

Today's Reading: Exodus 15:22-27

"Then Moses cried out to the LORD, and the LORD showed him a piece of wood. He threw it into the water, and the water became fit to drink" Exodus 15:25.

After the Israelites crossed the Red Sea, which God had miraculously divided allowing them to cross on dry ground, Moses led them into the Desert of Shur. They travelled for three days without finding any water, which made them quite unhappy. When they did find water, it was too bitter to drink. They grumbled to Moses. He turned to God for help, and God showed him a piece of wood and told him to throw it into the water which made it good to drink. Moses obeyed, and God supplied the need for sweet water. From there they went to a place that had twelve springs and seventy palm trees.

Author Leo Tolstoy wrote *"Everything comes in time to him who knows how to wait."* The Children of Israel didn't want to wait. They wanted a drink right then. We don't like to wait either. We want things to happen on our schedule. God has something wonderful for us, usually just around the corner, but waiting for it is the hard part. A friend of mine has a motto: *God gives the best to those who leave the choice to Him.* That's the hard part, leaving the choice to Him and waiting for it.

God had a wonderful place ahead for the Israelites, but they wanted water today. They were thirsty. Who can blame them? Three days without finding water must have been tough on people traveling on foot. God had just performed a supernatural miracle for them by parting the Red Sea and destroying Pharoah's army, all for their benefit. Now, just three days later, they're unhappy, discontented, grumbling. It seems they had forgotten for the moment the kind of God they were serving. In spite of their whining and grumbling, when Moses prayed, God gave them good water to drink and supplied a good camping spot.

If we're honest, most of us can admit to being a little like the Children of Israel— grumbling and complaining when things aren't like we want them. For the moment, it appears we have forgotten that God is faithful. He's always doing good things for us even when we grumble and complain. We just need to learn how to wait on Him.

Prayer: God, forgive my complaining and grumbling today. Help me to rely on You to give me water in the desert and to supply my needs on a daily basis. Amen.

Rahab: A Testimony of Water

Today's Reading: Joshua 2:1-22

"We have heard how the LORD dried up the water of the Red Sea for you when you came out of Egypt, and what you did to Sihon and Og, the two kings of the Amorites east of the Jordan, whom you completely destroyed" Joshua 2:10.

In October 1984, my husband had a heart catheterization at a large hospital in a city several miles away. During the procedure, one of his arteries was severed and they had to rush him to surgery immediately to save his life. God intervened that night, and he survived. We have told that testimony and I have written about it many times through the years. A lot of times when we tell it, people are shocked by what happened. When we share what God does in our lives, it will have an impact on others just as the story of God parting the Red Sea for the Israelites had an impact on people in that day.

When Joshua sent spies to spy out Jericho, they stayed in the house of a prostitute named Rahab. When they might have been captured, she hid them, keeping them safe. Afterwards, she said, "'We have heard how the Lord dried up the water of the Red Sea for you and what you did to the kings in the area.'" The testimony of what God had done for the Children of Israel reached other nations around them, and they were afraid of what God might do for His people when they came to Jericho. In fact, they were terrified.

"When we heard of it, our hearts melted in fear and everyone's courage failed because of you, for the LORD your God is God in heaven above and on the earth below" Joshua 2:11.

Sometimes we may feel our testimony will never reach anyone for God, but as we share it, we will never know just how far the Spirit of the Lord will carry our words and who will share it with someone else. Rahab had heard the testimony, and because she believed it, she and her whole family were saved when Israel invaded Jericho. For her, it meant life or death.

Keep sharing your testimony. It may save a life.

Prayer: God, give me the courage to share what You have done in my life that others may know of Your greatness and get to know You for themselves. Amen.

Vickie Phelps

Joshua: Stand in the Water

Today's Reading: 3:1-17

"Tell the priests who carry the ark of the covenant: 'When you reach the edge of the Jordan's waters, go and stand in the river'"
Joshua 3:8.

Near Milford, New Jersey, there is a floating barge on the Delaware River that sells hot dogs and burgers to hungry swimmers, boaters, and water tubers. To get to the food, you'll probably get wet though. You need to swim or tube out to the barge and then wait or stand in the river for your turn. If you're hungry, you probably won't mind the wait.

Before the battle of Jericho, God gave Joshua specific instructions for the people. They were to keep their eyes on the priests. When they saw the priests move out carrying the Ark of the Covenant, they were to follow them. They had never been this way before, but by watching the priests, they would know which way to go. "Joshua told the people, "Consecrate yourselves, for tomorrow the LORD will do amazing things among you" Joshua 3:5.

The priests had specific orders too. They were to go to the Jordan River and stand in it. As soon as their feet touched the water's edge the water flowing downstream would be shut off and would stand up in a heap. This provided a path on dry ground. The priests would remain standing in the water until all the people had passed through.

The people in this story all had their instructions to follow. As they followed what Joshua had told them to do, God worked on their behalf. He did amazing things for them.

God will do amazing things for us also, but we may have to stand in the middle of the river and wait for it to happen. I'm sure it took a while for all those Israelites to pass through to the other side. Did the priests get tired? Hungry? Thirsty? Wanted to do something else? Maybe yes to all those things. We also get tired or have something else we want to do when God calls on us to follow Him to the river. But if we stand in the water long enough, God will do amazing things in our lives.

Prayer: God, help me to keep my eyes on You, so I'll know when to move. Lead me to the

river and give me the strength to stand there until
You work out Your plan in my life. Amen.

Vickie Phelps

Noah: Saved by Water

Today's Reading: Genesis 6:13 through 7:16.

"For forty days the flood kept coming on the earth, and as the waters increased, they lifted the ark high above the earth. The waters rose and increased greatly on the earth, and the ark floated on the surface of the water" Genesis 7:17-18.

Suppose God asked you to build a boat or, in Noah's case, an ark. What would your answer be? For some it might be, "I don't know how to do that." Others might say, "Let someone else do it." A third answer in the twenty-first century would be "I don't have time." Not so for Noah. God said build an ark, and Noah did what God commanded him. Never mind that he had never built one before or might not have known what an ark was, he obeyed. God had specific instructions for Noah, and he followed them. If he hadn't, the ark might have sunk. Now consider these facts:

• Noah was not a young man; he was five hundred years old.

• It had never rained on earth before, so he had to take God at His word.

• It took him approximately one hundred years to build the ark.

• He did all the work without modern tools or technology.

• People probably mocked him while he worked.

None of these facts are encouraging, but Noah answered the call and finished the job. He made sure the animals entered the ark along with him and his family. Then it began to rain, a phenomenon that had never been witnessed before. Not a springtime shower or a summer thunderstorm. It rained water upon the earth until it covered everything and all life—human, animal, and plant—and drowned it except for Noah, his family, and the animals on board. Guess what? The ark floated. The same water that destroyed everything else lifted the ark and kept those inside safe.

Sometimes it feels like everything around us is falling apart. A flood of problems rains down on us. Our lives are chaotic to say the least. We lose our job, our car breaks down, a loved one passes away, a storm damages our home and on and on the list goes. Right in the middle of all this God asks us to do something for Him. Some of our answers may be the same scenario that Noah faced.

- We may think we're too old.
- We've never seen anything done like this before.
- It may take a long time to do it.
- We may not know how to use the tools we need to work with.
- We're afraid people will make fun of us.

If you could ask Noah today how he feels about all those things, I'm thinking he would say, "It doesn't matter. If I had let those things stop me, my family and I would have drowned."

The same water that destroyed everything else kept the ark afloat because Noah built it according to God's instructions, and he didn't let anything stop him. When we follow God's instructions, the waters of life won't pull us under. Our ark will float.

Prayer: Father, give me the courage and faith to follow your instructions as Noah did, doing all You ask of me and trusting You completely so my ship will float. Amen.

Hagar: Water in the Desert

Today's Reading: Genesis 21:1-21

"Then God opened her eyes and she saw a well of water. So she went and filled the skin with water and gave the boy a drink" Genesis 21:19.

Put yourself in Hagar's place. First, she was a slave to Sarah, catering to her needs, then Sarah decided to give her to Abraham, so she could conceive a child for them. Hagar didn't get a say in the matter. Second, once she had the child and weaned him, Sarah told Abraham to get rid of her and her son. Once again, she's at the whim of another woman who decides her fate. Abraham goes along with Sarah at God's instructions and sends Hagar and Ishmael away. She ends up wandering in the desert with limited resources. It was a desolate place—hot, dry, and dusty.

Hagar felt it was the end. They were out of water, and it was hot. She laid Ishmael under a bush and walked off a short distance. She didn't want to watch her son die. They both began to cry. Even though she felt they had nothing left, God heard their cries. The Angel of God told her not to be afraid. God opened her eyes, and she saw a well of water. They could drink now from the well God had provided. They would survive.

Sometimes we're faced with a situation that walks up and slaps us in the face. We're caught off balance. I'm sure Hagar felt that way when Abraham told her she and Ishmael would have to leave and go out on their own. She probably felt betrayed by the father of her son who provided for them. Suddenly, it's over. She has to go. A slap in the face for sure.

Are you in a desert today, wandering aimlessly without a destination in mind? Do you feel as though no one cares what happens to you? If life has slapped you in the face with an unbearable situation and you're wandering in a desolate landscape, don't give up. God hears you crying, and He will provide a way out even in the desert.

God is aware of your situation even though you may not see or hear anything at the moment. Keep crying out to Him. Hagar's and Ishmaels' sobs weren't in vain. God was listening. He's listening to you too. He has water in the desert for you.

Prayer: Lord, guide me through this desert I'm in. Hear my cries. Open my eyes and show me a well of water for my soul. Amen.

Vickie Phelps

Rebekah: A Bride-to-Be Draws Water

Today's Reading: Genesis 24:1-26

"After she had given him a drink, she said, "I'll draw water for your camels too, until they have had enough to drink" Genesis 24:19.

Marriage proposals can happen any place. Have you seen a man dropping to one knee in a public place and proposing to the woman of his choice? Maybe it was on a beach, during a halftime show at the big game, or in a restaurant, park, or on her front porch? It doesn't matter where it takes place as much as what her answer is. If the man down on one knee in front of her is the one she wants, she will say yes. She has a choice of whom she wants to marry.

Marriage proposals in Biblical times were quite different than our Western culture today. In Genesis 24 we read about Abraham asking his servant to find a wife for his son Isaac. Isaac didn't have a whole lot to say about it and neither did the young woman the servant would search for. The servant was to go to a certain region, find a suitable wife and bring her back. Isaac didn't get a chance to see her or spend time with her. It was all decided for him.

The obedient servant packed up his camels and left on his mission. When the servant reached his destination, he had his camels kneel beside the well where women came to draw water, then he prayed that God would direct the situation. He made a specific request about the woman—she would give him a drink of water and water his camels. By this he would know she was the right woman for Isaac. No sooner had he prayed than a woman bearing a water jar appeared. When he asked her for a drink, she gave him water. He didn't mention his camels, but the woman did. She offered to water his camels until they had enough to drink. Even though she knew nothing about the prayer the servant prayed, she went the extra mile. Without realizing it, she was the answer to his prayer. The simple act of giving the traveler a drink of water changed Rebekah's life forever. She could have ignored his request, but God was at work in this exchange between her and the servant.

Sometimes it's the routine trivial things in our lives that God uses to work out a problem or bring about the direction we so desperately need. We are looking for something big to happen, something wonderful, something magnificent— a supernatural miracle. And sometimes it does happen that way, but how many times has He used the small things, like a drink of water to bring about the answer to our need. Consider the small things in your life and watch for God to work.

Prayer: Lord, help me not to discredit the small things that can become big blessings in Your hands. Amen.

Pharaoh: Defeated by Water

Today's Reading: Exodus 14:1-29

"The water flowed back and covered the chariots and horsemen—the entire army of Pharaoh that had followed the Israelites into the sea. Not one of them survived" Exodus 14:28.

Pharoah was one determined man. He and his people suffered through several plagues before he finally told Moses to get out of Egypt and take the Israelites with him. But after they were gone, he started to rethink his decision and decided to pursue them. He assembled his army and off they went in hot pursuit of those Hebrews, but he was not prepared for what lay ahead.

On the other side, God was giving Moses' instructions for keeping the people safe from the enemy. When Moses stretched out his rod over the water, God caused a wind to blow all night and dry out the ground. A wall of water stood on each side, but the Israelites walked across without harm. Pharoah sent his army in after them. Once again, God told Moses to stretch out his rod over the sea, and the water returned to its place covering the Egyptian army, drowning them in defeat.

Do you ever feel like the enemy is hot on your trail? Every way you turn he is there attempting to drag you back to the old life or wreck the new one you're building. If it isn't you he's following, it's one of your family members or a close friend. No matter how many times you attempt to lose him, he keeps riding on your bumper, trying to force you off the road. I am sure the Israelites felt the same way. In fact, they even accused Moses of trying to get them killed by leading them out of Egypt and into the wilderness. Moses said, "The LORD will fight for you; you need only to be still." Exodus 14:14.

The Israelites didn't even have to draw a sword or get into battle formation. All they had to do was stand still and watch. Those walls of water moved back into place and the entire enemy army drowned.

Whenever Satan is pursuing you, remember that God can stop him in his tracks just as He did the Egyptian army. Our part is to be still and allow the Lord to fight for us. And that is the hard part at times. To our way of thinking, being still is counterproductive. We want to jump in and take care of things. Too often, we try to fight the battle alone. Stand still today and watch to see what God will do for you.

Prayer: God, help me to listen when you tell me to stand still. Calm my spirit so that I won't be fretting and wanting to jump into the fight. Help me to trust You to fight for me. Amen.

Vickie Phelps

Joseph: No Water in the Cistern

Today's Reading: Genesis 37:1-36

"So when Joseph came to his brothers, they stripped him of his robe—the ornate robe he was wearing—and they took him and threw him into the cistern. The cistern was empty; there was no water in it" Genesis 37:23-24.

Joseph, a dreamer, and a favored child by Jacob, his father, was thrown into a cistern by his own brothers. That was bad enough in itself, but they also stripped him of the robe his father had given him and conspired to lie to their father. Their jealousy knew no bounds. Fortunately for Joseph, the cistern was empty. If it had been full of water, he might have drowned. Even so, I'm sure that empty cistern was not a pleasant place. Was it cold, smelly, home to snakes or other creatures?

We can make all the plans we want, have big dreams, and work toward them, and then without warning, things fall apart, and we feel like we've ended up in an empty cistern. It may not be pleasant, but God has something better waiting for us. He won't force it on us. We're not puppets on His strings, but He knows what's best and when we follow His plan, success is following close behind. Even though Joseph was sold to a band of travelers going to Egypt, it was in the right direction. We're not told what Joseph was feeling or said to his brothers as he was carried away, but he was on his way to better things. He just didn't know it.

If we follow God, we're on our way to better things. What kind of things? We can rest assured that He knows how to give good gifts to His children. In James chapter one we read, "Don't be deceived, my dear brothers and sisters. Every good and perfect gift is from above, coming down from the Father of the heavenly lights, who does not change like shifting shadows" James 1:16-17. And when we commit our plans to Him, Proverbs 16:3 says He will establish our plans.

Joseph was in a dry cistern one day, sold as a slave the next day, lied on, and thrown into prison on another day but became number two man in the land of Egypt, second only to Pharoah according to God's plan. Only God can take us from the bottom to the top in that kind of order. Joseph faced many obstacles in his journey, but he overcame them to receive the best of everything in the end. We can expect the best from God.

Prayer: God, help me to trust You even in the dry cisterns of my life. Amen.

Vickie Phelps

Jonah: "Throw Me in The Water."

Today's Reading: Jonah 1:1-17.

"Pick me up and throw me into the sea," he replied, "and it will become calm. I know that it is my fault that this great storm has come upon you" Jonah 1:12.

Has God ever asked you to do something you did not want to do? For one reason or another you wished he would choose someone else. Was it because you felt unqualified or had something else you would rather do? Or you simply didn't want the task because you felt it was beneath you? Ouch.

Jonah found himself in this same situation when God asked him to go to Nineveh and preach. He did not want to go preach to those heathens, so he bought a ticket for Tarshish and took off, thinking he could hide from God. He boarded a ship and found a place to sleep. At some point a storm came up, and the ship was in danger of breaking up. When they woke him, they told him to pray.

Jonah knew why they were in danger. This storm was one of his own making. He admitted he served the God that created the heavens. He told them to throw him overboard, so they could be saved. He thought his fate was drowning, but God had other plans. He already had the fish prepared to save Jonah.

It is impossible to hide from God. When He asks us to do something, obedience should be our only response. If we don't obey, we may face fierce storms that toss us around and bring destruction. Like Jonah, these storms may come because of our decisions or actions.

Are we courageous enough to ask God to throw us overboard into the middle of what He has planned for us? Are we repentant enough to admit we made a mistake? Is our faith strong enough to let God be in control? Jonah expected to drown. Instead, God had the fish waiting, ready to swallow Jonah, preserving his life. Jonah didn't like being in the belly of that fish. He called it the realm of the dead. The King James Version describes it as the belly of hell. Either way, it was not a pleasant place, but he called on God. He repented, and God delivered him from the fish. Now Jonah was ready to obey.

We don't know what will happen if we get thrown into the water, but we can trust God to take care of the situation. We might not like the way He does it, but it is always for our best.

What will it take for us to get in the place where God wants us?

Prayer: God, when the storms come and I end up getting thrown overboard, save me for your purposes. Give me an obedient heart to follow where you lead. Amen.

Naaman: "I want Clean Water."

Today's Reading: 2 Kings 5:1-14.

"Are not Abana and Pharpar, the rivers of
Damascus, better than all the waters of Israel?
Couldn't I wash in them and be cleansed?" So,
he turned and went off in a rage" 2 Kings 5:12.

Naaman was a highly regarded
commander for the Syrian army—a
hero of sorts. He had been victorious in
battle and even his master thought of him as a
great man. He had it good except for one thing.
He had leprosy. In Biblical times, it was seen as
a curse or a sign of sin or uncleanness. In his
position as an important military man, Naaman
needed healing. His wife had a maid who was a
captive from Israel. She told her mistress if
Naaman would go see the prophet in Samaria, he

could heal him. Naaman received permission to go, so off he went. But when he finally arrived, Elisha, the prophet, didn't even come out to greet him. He sent a messenger to tell Naaman to go wash in the Jordan River.

Guess what? This leprous man took offense at being addressed by a mere messenger. He thought the prophet should have come out and spoken with a great man like himself. And that prophet had the nerve to tell him to go wash in that muddy, silt filled Jordan River when there were better rivers around. His pride was hurt.

Thank goodness, Naaman had some wise servants who spoke to him and said if he had been asked to do something great, he would have done it. All he had to do was go dip in the Jordan River. Was that a hard thing? No, it might not have been the most glamorous river to take a dip in, but it was the one God used. When Naaman put aside his pride and stepped into that muddy river, healing happened.

Who among us hasn't told God we know exactly how things should be done? In other words, we don't want to be behind-the-scenes. We want some recognition, and we don't want to get our hands dirty or break a manicured nail in the process. We don't want to swim in a muddy river. We want to choose our own river. We want to talk to the prophet himself and have him recognize us and lay hands on us.

It's only when we realize that our pride is keeping us from receiving what God has for us and we become willing to step into whatever muddy river God is indicating, that we begin to see healing take place. What river are you standing in?

Prayer: God, show me the pride that keeps me from receiving from You and help me step into the river You have chosen. Amen.

Vickie Phelps

Gideon: A Bowlful of Water

Today's Reading: Judges 6

"Gideon said to God, "If you will save Israel by my hand as you have promised—look, I will place a wool fleece on the threshing floor. If there is dew only on the fleece and all the ground is dry, then I will know that you will save Israel by my hand, as you said." And that is what happened. Gideon rose early the next day; he squeezed the fleece and wrung out the dew—a bowlful of water" Judges 6:36-38.

More than once, I have put a fleece before God, not because I didn't trust Him, but I needed an answer or direction. I wanted to be sure it came from God. Sometimes we're not sure of ourselves, and we must have the reassurance that we're doing the right thing. You know the routine. "God, if you'll do this certain thing, I'll know it's from You," or "Let this happen and I'll know what You want me to do." Sound familiar? We're not alone. Gideon needed an answer to his problem too.

The first thing the angel of God said to Gideon was "the Lord is with you mighty warrior." If that had been me, I would have looked around to see if someone else had entered the room. My response might have been "Are you talking to me?" Gideon felt much the same way. He didn't see himself as a mighty warrior. In fact, a few verses down he declares, "I am the least in my family." In other words, you have the wrong man. There are others much better suited for the job.

God assured Gideon that He was with him, and he would be victorious, but that wasn't quite enough for Gideon. Sometimes I've been a Gideon. I know what God's Word says but I want to be convinced beyond any doubt. That doubt may come from my feeling insecure that I can do what God is requesting of me, or it may be a question of knowing God's voice when I hear it. Gideon felt the same. In verse 17, he says, "give me a sign that it is really you talking to me." Then he made his request known.

God answered Gideon by giving him a wet fleece. The fleece wasn't just wet, it was soaked, so much so that he squeezed a bowlful of water from it. He did this not once, but twice to be sure of God's answer. Only this time he asked that the fleece be dry and the ground wet. God answered once again with water.

If we set out a dry fleece and ask for a wet one, we should expect to see water as a result. Will it be a bowlful? That part is up to God. Who knows, it could be a bucketful. When we trust God for an answer, we can expect to get one. He will answer us in such a way that doubt will have to flee.

Prayer: God, give me the confidence to trust You and Your answers. Amen.

Vickie Phelps

Samson: Refreshed by Water

Today's Reading: Judges 15:1-20

"Then God opened up the hollow place in Lehi, and water came out of it. When Samson drank, his strength returned, and he revived" Judges 15:19.

Samson was angry. His father-in-law had given his wife to another man, so he retaliated by burning the grain fields, the olive groves, and the vineyards of the Philistines. When they found out Samson's reason for doing so, the Philistines then took their revenge on the father-in-law and Samson's wife and burned them to death. In retaliation, Samson killed many of the Philistines.

Because of his actions, three thousand men from his own country of Judah came to arrest him and turn him over to the Philistines. He allowed himself to be bound and taken but as he approached Lehigh, the Philistines came toward him shouting. The Spirit of the Lord came upon Samson. He broke the cords which bound him and killed a thousand Philistines with the jawbone of a donkey. Afterwards, he was weak and needed water.

"Because he was very thirsty, he cried out to the LORD, "You have given your servant this great victory. Must I now die of thirst and fall into the hands of the uncircumcised?" (Verse 18). God heard his cry for water and opened a spring just for Samson. The water revived him, and his strength returned.

Nothing tastes better than a drink of cold water when you're hot, tired, and thirsty. It revives you and gives you strength to continue. It is just as important that we drink spiritual water to keep us revived. How many times has God provided spiritual water for you when you were thirsty? When the battle gets long, and you are weary with life and fighting each day to keep going, a drink from His fountain will give you fresh life. As you spend time talking with Him and reading His Word, you will receive the strength you need to continue fighting the battle. God will open a spring of water just for you. Samson revived and went on to lead the people of Israel for twenty years. Who knows what God may lead you to do when you drink from his spring?

Prayer: God, open a spring of Your water today. Revive me and refresh me so I can continue in the battle. Amen.

Elisha: Pools of Water

Today's Reading: 2 Kings 3:1-26

"While the harpist was playing, the hand of the LORD came on Elisha and he said, "This is what the LORD says: I will fill this valley with pools of water. For this is what the LORD says: You will see neither wind nor rain, yet this valley will be filled with water, and you, your cattle and your other animals will drink" 2 Kings 3:16-17.

Three kings, the king of Israel, the king of Judah, and the king of Edom set out to fight against the king of Moab who had rebelled against the king of Israel. They decided to attack through the desert of Edom but after a roundabout march of seven days, they were out of water. They were at a loss as to what to do, but they decided to call on Elisha, a prophet of God for an answer.

God gave the three kings an answer. Where there had been no water, He would fill the valley with pools of water. They wouldn't see a storm of any kind, no wind or rain, and yet water would be standing all around them. Where would the water come from if it didn't rain. God, of course. Not only would they have water, but He would deliver the enemy king into their hands.

If you're in a battle and you run out of water, call on God. He can give you pools of water where you had none before. If the enemy is coming against you and you need reinforcements, call on God. Water from God will sustain you.

Prayer: God, send me water, pools of water. Fill this valley I'm in, so I can quench my thirst and defeat the enemy.

David: Give Me a Drink of Water

Today's Reading: 1 Chronicles 11:1-19

"David longed for water and said, "Oh, that someone would get me a drink of water from the well near the gate of Bethlehem!" 1 Chronicles 11:17.

In December 1944, Lieutenant John Robert Fox, an artillery officer was fighting the Nazis in Italy. The Nazis had overrun a small village in Tuscany and Americans were in retreat. Fox asked for artillery fire to be directed at the village to give the US forces time to regroup and launch a counterattack. He ordered a barrage of fire on his exact position. The gunner who received the message assumed it must be a mistake. Fox, however, simply said: "Fire it. There's more of them than there are us."

His sacrifice gave the allies a chance to regroup and launch a successful counterattack. He made the ultimate sacrifice for the others.[4]

David found himself in a similar situation in a battle with the Philistines. He was in a stronghold at the cave Adullam, and the Philistines were in a stronghold at Bethlehem, David's birthplace. Thirsty and weary from the battle and thinking about that good, sweet water from Bethlehem, he longed for a drink from that well. When he voiced his wish aloud, three of his mighty warriors broke through the Philistine stronghold and obtained water for David. They didn't do it without risk to their own safety. They were courageous men who had to fight their way to that well. The scripture says they broke through the Philistine stronghold. When they returned and gave David the water, he realized the risk his men had taken for him so he could have a drink. It was a testimony to their loyalty and love for David, but he couldn't drink the water. It was too precious knowing what it took to obtain it. He poured it out as an offering

---

[4] https://historycollection.com/10-of-the-most-heroic-acts-of-self-sacrifice-in-history/2/

to the Lord.

Knowing the sacrifice Jesus made for us at Calvary should make it more precious to us each day. The enemy thought he had gotten rid of Jesus, but Jesus arose victoriously and ascended to the Father. He broke through the enemy stronghold and provided salvation. He gave His all that we might live. Pour out an offering of praise and thanksgiving to Him for giving His all on our behalf.

Prayer: Jesus, thank You for the sacrifice You made for me on the cross. Help me never to lose sight of how precious it is. Amen.

Vickie Phelps

Elijah: A Watery Sacrifice

Today's Reading: 1 Kings 18:16-39

"Then the fire of the LORD fell and burned up
the sacrifice, the wood, the stones, and the soil,
and also licked up the water in the trench.
When all the people saw this, they fell prostrate
and cried, "The LORD—he is God! The
LORD—he is God!" 1Kings 18:38-39.

Several years ago, we lived in the country.
Some neighbors across the road built a
beautiful log house. One evening while
watching T.V. we heard a strange crackling
sound, and my husband went to investigate the
noise. To his amazement, the log house was on
fire. We hurried over where people had already
begun to congregate. The owners stood outside
the house watching it burn. A fire truck arrived,

but spraying water on the fire had no effect. The house burned to the ground. The fire was too powerful.

The Old Testament prophet, Elijah, had his own fire—a sacrifice to God to prove to King Ahab and the people that God is the one true God. Elijah said, "How long will you waver between two opinions? If the LORD is God, follow him; but if Baal is God, follow him." After the followers of Baal had made a sacrifice to their god and gone through all their pagan rituals which included cutting their bodies until they bled, Elijah repaired the altar of God which had been torn down. He dug a trench around the altar and prepared the sacrifice. He then commanded that water be poured over the sacrifice. This was done three more times until water ran down around the altar and filled the trench.

When Elijah called on God, fire fell from heaven, burned up the sacrifice, the wood, the stones, and the soil, and licked up the water in the trench. This wasn't just any fire; it was holy fire from God—powerful fire that could lick up water. In the natural world, water helps extinguish fire, but in this case, fire extinguished the water. The people recognized that God is indeed the one and only true God.

When circumstances around us look impossible, we need to remember that we serve a God who can change the natural state of things. As humans, we use our knowledge and education to figure out the most reasonable solution to problems. Sometimes we must settle for what we consider less than the best, but God calls what man thinks is not a possibility as though it had already happened. We can trust Him to turn things around and settle for something greater. He is the one true God.

Prayer: God, send down Your Holy fire, burn up the carnal things in my life and turn the impossible into the possible. Amen.

Daniel: Water Not Wine

Today's Reading: Daniel 1:1-21:

"Please test your servants for ten days: Give us nothing but vegetables to eat and water to drink" Daniel 1:12.

Daniel and three of his friends were captives in Babylon. The king was grooming them to enter his service. They were to learn the language and the literature of the Babylonians. In addition, they were to eat from the king's table. Daniel did not want to defile himself by eating and drinking the king's food. He was Jewish, and they had their own dietary laws.

He challenged the court official whom he had found favor with, to let him eat vegetables instead of the king's food and to drink water instead of the king's wine for ten days. It was risky because it could cost the official his life. He finally agreed to let Daniel have his way. At the end of the ten days, Daniel and his friends looked healthier than any of the other men who had eaten the king's food. Verse seventeen reads: "To these four young men God gave knowledge and understanding of all kinds of literature and learning. And Daniel could understand visions and dreams of all kinds."

When we feed on the delicacies the world has to offer, we will miss out on what God has for us, and we will soon begin to have an unhealthy lifestyle and attitude. What we take into our bodies, both physically and spiritually, affects our health. When we receive the food and water of God's Spirit, we will be healthy and live flourishing spiritual lives.

Prayer: God, Take away my desire for the delicacies of the world. Give me food and water from Your storehouse that I may be a healthy Christian in the kingdom of God. Amen.

The Impotent Man: Moving Water

Today's Reading: John 5:1-14

"Sir," the invalid replied, "I have no one to help
me into the pool when the water is stirred.
While I am trying to get in, someone else goes
down ahead of me" John 5:7.

Jesus made a trip to Jerusalem and while
there He encountered an impotent man
lying beside the Pool of Bethesda. At
certain times of the year, an angel came and
troubled the waters of that pool and the person
who stepped into the water first after the
troubling was healed of whatever disease they
had. (Verse 4, KJV). The scripture says the man
had been in this condition for thirty-eight years.
He had no one to help him into the water, but he
was about to meet the one who could change his

life forever.

Jesus asked a question: "Do you want to get well?" The man answered, "I have no one to help me and when I'm trying to get in, someone steps in before me."

That must have been a very discouraging situation to find oneself in day after day. No matter how hard he tried to get there, he just wasn't fast enough or strong enough. No one around him was concerned enough to help him. Until Jesus came by.

Jesus said, "Get up! Pick up your mat and walk."

This said to a man who could not stand alone, who would have had difficulty bending over to pick up anything. Now he was being told to stand, bend over, pick up his mat, and walk all in one fell swoop. The man was healed instantly. He didn't need to get into the pool. He didn't need someone to pick him up or support him to the water. Jesus came by. That's all it took.

Have you ever felt you were sitting on the edge of a new life, a better chance or the answer to an old problem but couldn't seem to get over the hurdle by yourself? No one stops to help you. You struggle to get ahead, but before you can take the next step, someone jumps in ahead of you. It seems everyone around you is getting blessed while you're still sitting on the sidelines. Don't give up, all you need is for Jesus to come by. Don't quit praying or asking for the answer. Keep waiting. Sometimes the waiting game is difficult, but you never know when He's coming so don't give up.

Prayer: Jesus, please walk by my situation. Stop and give me the instructions I need to receive my answer. Amen.

Peter: Walking on Water

Today's Reading: Matthew 14:14-33
"But when he saw the wind, he was afraid and beginning to sink, cried out, "Lord, save me!" Matthew 14:30.

I once thought myself brave enough to ride a rollercoaster, not just any old rollercoaster but a high one that climbed forever and dropped suddenly. Other people looked like they were having a grand time flying around on that track, so I got in line. I found out I wasn't as brave as I thought. By the time we reached the top and I knew what was going to happen, I told the Lord if He would get me off, I would never get on it again.

We can all relate to a time when we have been terrified because of a scary situation. Your heart pounds, chills crawl over you and you wonder if you're going to get out of the situation, or if this is it for you or someone you care about.

Whenever the disciples saw Jesus walking on the water, they were terrified until they realized who He was. Peter said, "Lord, if it's you, tell me to come to you on the water." Jesus said, "Come." Peter climbed out of the boat. I don't think he was afraid of the water in the beginning. He was a fisherman. He had spent many days on the water; it was familiar territory to him. The Bible doesn't tell us what Peter was thinking that first moment his foot touched the water. He just started walking toward Jesus. What a thrill to experience walking on top of water. All went well until he looked around him and saw the wind blowing and the water rolling. Scripture doesn't tell us that noise was a part of the scene, but storms are noisy, so if you throw in the possibility of roaring wind and waves, then he could not only see but hear the storm. It would be easy to become distracted. Peter became afraid and began to sink. In that moment of terror, he cried out to Jesus for help, and immediately Jesus reached out and caught him.

Whenever Jesus rescued Peter, he asked him a question. "Why did you doubt?" We don't know what Peter said in response, maybe nothing, but from the question Jesus asked, I think the key to successful water walking is "don't doubt." Keep your eyes on Jesus and believe that He can keep you above water no matter how rough the wind gets or how high the waves are. If you start looking at the world around you, and listening to all the noise it makes, it may cause you to take your eyes off Jesus. If you do become afraid, call on the one who is the Master of the wind and water. Jesus will reach out and take your hand and pull you to safety.

Prayer: Lord, help me to keep my eyes on You and my ears open to Your voice. Help me to lose interest in those things that would distract me from getting to You. Amen.

Vickie Phelps

Paul: In Deep Water

Today's Reading: Acts 27

"After they had gone a long time without food, Paul stood up before them and said: "Men, you should have taken my advice not to sail from Crete; then you would have spared yourselves this damage and loss. But now I urge you to keep up your courage, because not one of you will be lost; only the ship will be destroyed" Acts 27:21-22.

Have you ever wished you had taken someone's advice and not jumped into a decision of your own too quickly? Most of us have made mistakes which could have been avoided if we had listened to someone else. If the men in our reading today had taken Paul's advice, they wouldn't have faced shipwreck and ended up swimming for their lives or floating in deep water.

Paul had advised them that the voyage would be disastrous with the loss of the ship and some lives, but the centurion traveling with them listened to the ship's pilot and owner. He probably thought Paul didn't know what he was talking about. After all, he was a prisoner. His words didn't carry too much weight.

It's amazing how we apply importance to people's advice based on who or what they are, and sometimes that's a good thing. But often, the most unlikely individuals have more wisdom and knowledge than some who are thought to be on a different social, educational, or financial level. In Numbers 22, God used a donkey to relay a message to its owner. "Then the LORD opened the donkey's mouth, and it said to Balaam, "What have I done to you to make you beat me these three times?" If God can use a donkey, then he can use anyone to carry out His plans.

Even though the men aboard ship with Paul didn't listen to his advice, God gave Paul a message of encouragement letting him know that he would still appear before Caesar, and they would all be saved. The centurion would have done well to listen to Paul. They lost their cargo. The ship broke up during the storm and the men aboard ended up in the water either swimming to shore or clinging to wooden planks or other parts of the ship to stay afloat. God was merciful, and every man survived but how much better if they had listened to Paul and saved the ship and cargo.

We can take a lesson from Paul's story. When God has a message for us, we would do well to listen. He may speak to us himself, but He may send the message through someone else in a sermon, scripture, or wise advice. Are we willing to listen to that person knowing that God can use whomever He chooses, even a donkey.

Prayer: Lord, keep my ears open to Your voice no matter who You choose to send it through. Help me to accept the messenger from You as well as the message. Amen.

Water Psalms

The book of Psalms is a treasure trove of songs, prayers, and instruction to the reader. David, the Sweet Singer of Israel, is the author of many of the psalms. He is often raising his voice in praise to God but many times he is crying out to God for help. Asaph, another skilled singer and poet, also wrote psalms of praise and prayer.

The subject of water shows up often in the book of Psalms. Sometimes the writer speaks of himself and his circumstances as he does in Psalm 119:136: "Streams of tears flow from my eyes, for your law is not obeyed." Sometimes the writer is referring to the magnificence of God and His power over water as he does in Psalm 93:4: "Mightier than the thunder of the great waters, mightier than the breakers of the sea— the LORD on high is mighty."

No matter which one of the psalms we read, we will find God a central part of the writing whether being praised or called on for help. I think we can all relate to that.

Planted by the Water

Today's Reading: Psalm 1

"That person is like a tree planted by streams of water, which yields its fruit in season and whose leaf does not wither—whatever they do prospers" Psalm 1:3.

My husband has a green thumb. He can stick a twig in a pot of dirt or in the ground and before you know it, he has a little tree growing. He babies and waters and takes care of that small creation until it's large enough to be planted in the ground. His care doesn't stop there though. He continues to take care of it until it can survive on its own in the elements, but he always makes sure it has plenty of water even when it reaches maturity. Because of his watering, we enjoy fruit, beauty, and shade from what he plants.

Water is essential to the growth and

production of a tree. Deep roots help trees absorb more water and nutrients from the soil. They also act as an anchor, helping the tree to stay upright in the wind. Those roots search for water, sometimes going hundreds of feet down to find the nourishment they need. They will even climb through cracks in cement.

In today's reading the Psalmist states that the person who watches where he walks, stands and sits is blessed. He is sending us a message loud and clear. Don't take on the characteristics of the ungodly world around you. Be careful of standing where sinners are standing. They may be in a place of evil and harm. Do not sit with the scornful who sneer at others and have a superior attitude. The characteristics of these people will only bring you trouble, pain, and ruin, causing you to wither.

The person who meditates on God's Word flourishes. Like a tree planted close to the water whose roots seek out the source of nourishment it needs, we should seek out God's plan for us through His Word, allowing nothing to stop our progress in our search for water from God. As we sink our roots deep into His law and take delight in it, we will flourish and produce fruit.

Prayer: Father, give me deep roots that I can sink into your Word and draw nourishing water from your laws. Help me to push forward in my search for more of you regardless of the obstacles in my way. Amen.

Deep Water

Today's Reading: Psalm 18:1-19

"He reached down from on high and took hold of me; he drew me out of deep waters" Psalm 18:16.

David is said to have sung this song when the Lord delivered him from the hands of his enemies and King Saul. He had been on the run for his life because of King Saul's jealousy. He must have felt as if he were swimming around in those deep waters with no way out until the Lord took hold of him and drew him out.

David's story started at a young age. Samuel showed up at his father, Jesse's house with a horn of oil. David was out tending sheep at the time but when all his brothers were passed over by God, Samuel asked if there were any more brothers. "Only the youngest who is out with the sheep," Jesse told him.

"Send for him," Samuel said.

When David came in, the Lord spoke to Samuel and said, "He's the one." Samuel anointed him that day to be King over Israel, but it was several years before David ascended to the throne. King Saul's jealousy kept him running and hiding for his life for a long time. I am sure that there were times in David's life when he wondered why these things were happening to him. He was God's chosen man.

Sometimes we as believers wonder why trouble comes when we're trying our best to do the right thing. We have been made a part of God's family by the blood of Jesus. We're living and working for Him. So why me, Lord? Even though we're God's children, we live in a sinful world, and we're not exempt from the effects of the world around us just as David wasn't. And just like David, God will reach down and lift us out of the deep waters we're swimming around in. All we have to do is trust Him. David trusted God to keep His promises, and the day came when David ascended to the throne and became king.

Prayer: Father, give me the perseverance I need to trust You to lift me out of the deep waters in my life. Amen.

Beside Quiet Waters

Today's Reading: Psalm 23

"The LORD is my shepherd, I lack nothing. He makes me lie down in green pastures, he leads me beside quiet waters, he refreshes my soul" Psalm 23:1-3.

As a shepherd, David knew the importance of quiet waters. Sheep are afraid of rushing water and will hesitate to approach it. They look for quiet water to drink from. Rushing water can also be dangerous for them. If they fall in and their wool gets wet, it becomes heavy, and they can drown. David took care of his father's sheep by making sure they had good water to drink and fighting off bears and lions to keep them safe.

When David penned this psalm, he was thinking of the Lord and how he is like a good shepherd to his people. As our shepherd, Jesus is all we need. He cares for us, making sure of our safety and comfort. When we're weary and stressed, He can give us a quietness in our spirit, a peace no one else can give. Paul, writing to the Philippian church said these words: "And the peace of God, which transcends all understanding, will guard your hearts and your minds in Christ Jesus" Philippians 4:7. When we are faced with trouble or danger, and we remain calm in our spirit, we know that peace is not of ourselves, but comes from God.

When a car plowed through the front of my place of employment headed in my direction, I wondered if this was the end, if it would be my last day to live, but I felt no fear. A great peace came over me while all around me chaos reigned. I was safe in the arms of the shepherd. He had led me to quiet waters, and I came away unharmed. I had no doubt in my mind I had experienced that peace Paul had written about.

If you watch the evening news, you will see a world full of unrest, pain, and evil. It can be disturbing to see all that's happening around us. If we dwell on these things, it will destroy our peace. It will lead us away from the quiet waters the Lord has provided for us. That doesn't mean we aren't concerned for the people in trouble, but when circumstances are beyond our control, we can leave it in God's hands and rest in His green pastures beside His quiet waters.

Prayer: Lord, guide me to quiet waters today. Help me to center my thoughts on you and experience the kind of peace only you can give. Amen.

Vickie Phelps

The Sea in Jars

Today's Reading: Psalm 33

"By the word of the LORD the heavens were made, their starry host by the breath of his mouth. He gathers the waters of the sea into jars; he puts the deep into storehouses. Let all the earth fear the LORD; let all the people of the world revere him. For he spoke, and it came to be; he commanded, and it stood firm" Psalm 33: 6-9.

It is impossible to describe God. We may have a large vocabulary and know how to use many words. Yet when you try to describe who God is, it's hard to find words wonderful enough to paint the picture you want others to see. In his book, "*The Treasury of David*, "Charles Spurgeon writes: *"The sweetest tunes, the sweetest voices, and the sweetest words are all too little for the Lord our God."*

The only one powerful enough to gather the sea into jars and the deep into storehouses is our sovereign God. Think about that for a moment. Can you even imagine that happening? And all it takes is a word from Him to make these magnificent waters come together and keep their boundaries. "The sea that invades the shore under the impulse of the moon would devour the land if a divine decree did not maintain its bounds."[5]

Prayer: God, I worship You in the best way I know how by giving You the glory and the credit for all of creation. You are the magnificent creator of all we know and see. Amen.

---

[5] *The Treasury of David*, Charles Haddon Spurgeon ©1997, Thomas Nelson, Inc.

Panting for Water

Today's Reading: Psalm 42

"As the deer pants for streams of water, so my soul pants for you, my God." Psalm 42:1.

Our little schnauzer loves to run and play with the dogs on the other side of the fence. Even though the fence keeps each of them in their own yards, they can peer through the cracks at each other and chase up and down the yard. Sometimes she comes in the house with her tongue hanging out, panting hard, headed straight for her water dish. She knows what will revive her and cool her tongue and throat.

As a girl growing up, I played outside a lot. I was the typical tomboy who loved baseball games and climbing trees. There were several kids in our neighborhood, and we spent a lot of time in the sun. Texas summers are hot and long. When our tongues were hanging out and we were thirsty, we ran for the water hose. Nothing tasted or felt as good as that water bubbling up out of the end of that hose. It was a lifesaver for us on those long summer days. Just as we need water for our physical bodies, we need spiritual water for our spirit.

The writer expressed his spiritual thirst by saying he panted after God. In other words, he was saying he was running, breathing hard, his tongue might be hanging out as he pursued after God. He wanted a spiritual drink, and he knew the source. He wanted it badly enough that he exerted himself to obtain that drink. In his book, *The Treasury of David*," Charles Spurgeon wrote, *"When it is as natural to long for God as an animal longs to drink, it is well with our souls however painful our feelings."*

The world holds many things we can pant after, but they won't satisfy our spiritual thirst. Do we want God enough to exert ourselves? Are we willing to run until we're breathing hard and panting to get more of Him in our lives? Are we thirsty for a spiritual drink from God?

Prayer: God, make me thirsty for more of You. Help me to run after You until I receive the spiritual drink I need. Amen.

Roaring Waters

Today's Reading: Psalm 46

"God is our refuge and strength, an ever-present help in trouble. Therefore we will not fear, though the earth give way and the mountains fall into the heart of the sea, though its waters roar and foam and the mountains quake with their surging" Psalm 46:1-3.

Have you ever stood next to a fast-moving river as it rolls and tumbles toward its destination or been to Niagara Falls and heard the roar of the falling water? You wouldn't think something as clear and natural as water could be so noisy, and yet it can roar so loudly you can hardly hear the person standing next to you.

The psalmist writes of the earth giving way

and mountains falling into the sea, roaring waters and quaking mountains. All of these things can be frightening but he's not going to fear. His trust is in God. He has complete confidence in God as a refuge, source of strength, and ever-present help.

Nature is full of powerful forces that can wreak havoc on the earth. Watching the news and seeing the devastation caused by tornadoes, hurricanes, floods and earthquakes gives us an idea of just how powerful these elements are and yet, our God controls these forces. He can hold back these mighty forces with His hand. He can stop them in the middle of their raging and bring peace.

Like the psalmist, our confidence rests in God—His power, His mighty acts, and His unfailing love for His children.

Prayer: God, I praise You for Your creation and all its beauty and Your power to control all the mighty forces of nature. Amen.

Thirsty for Water

Today's Reading: Psalm 63

"You, God, are my God, earnestly I seek you; I thirst for you, my whole being longs for you, in a dry and parched land where there is no water." Psalm 63:1.

Merriam Webster defines thirsty as "having a strong desire for something." You notice it does not mention the word water in the definition. That's because we can feel a thirst or a desire for something besides water. In the search to quench our thirst, we might grab the first liquid we encounter which makes us feel better for a time but later, we may still feel the need for a simple glass or bottle of water. Things don't always satisfy like we expect them to.

Remember the story of David in one of the earlier devotions? He wanted a drink from the well of Bethlehem. He had a strong desire for the water from his hometown. He was thirsty for only that water. He could almost taste it. He wanted it badly, but when he realized the risk taken to get it, he couldn't drink it.

Sometimes we have such a strong desire for something we can almost taste it but once we have it in our hands or at least within reach, it doesn't always look as good as we thought it would. It doesn't always satisfy us or fill the need we expected it to. What you and I desire should quench the thirst we feel inside, or we will find ourselves perpetually thirsty, never satisfied, never having our need quenched. The big question is what are we thirsty for?

The world around us holds many enticements for all of us. There are a lot of things we can reach for, maybe even thirst for, but will they satisfy us, or will it be a temporary sip of something that leaves us feeling empty and unfulfilled? The Psalmist said he was thirsty for God; his whole being longed for Him. He was in a dry, parched place, no water present but even with the absence of water, he was thirsty for God.

When you are hot and thirsty, what is your reaction to a glass of water? Do you take a little sip and let it go or do you turn the glass up and gulp down a mouthful? Have you ever watched sports on T.V.? Sometimes the players grab a bottle of water and chug down the whole thing or pour half of it over their head, anything to refresh themselves.

When you're spiritually dry, parched, and need refreshing, do you long for God's presence? When you pray, are you a sipper or a gulper? Do you feel you can get by on a few swallows? When He makes Himself known to us, do we drink until we're running over? It's only when we drink His spiritual water that our thirst will be quenched.

Prayer: God, make me thirsty for You. Help me to long for the spiritual water You provide, not just a sip, but enough to fill my spirit and pour over my head also. Amen.

Vickie Phelps

Watered by God

Today's Reading: Psalm 65

"You care for the land and water it; you enrich it abundantly. The streams of God are filled with water to provide the people with grain, for so you have ordained it. You drench its furrows and level its ridges; you soften it with showers and bless its crops" Psalm 65:9-10.

When I married my husband, he had what appeared to me to be a ball of brown twigs in a plastic container. Left to my own devices, I might have thrown it away, thinking it was something dead, but he explained to me that all he had to do was pour water on it and it would come to life. Within a few minutes I watched in amazement as the plant started opening and spreading out. It was my first encounter with a resurrection plant. His mother had given it to him when he was a young man in his twenties. The plant is now more than sixty years old but today after it had been sitting on a shelf in his shop for quite a while my husband poured water on it, and it began to unfold and open. These plants can survive for long periods of time in a dehydrated state but once they get even a little water, they come to life.

Have you ever noticed the difference a refreshing rain makes in the life around us? Where there has been dry, withering vegetation, new life seems to spring out of the dryness. We can water our garden with a sprinkler and hose to keep it alive, but nothing revives it like a good rain. God cares about the earth He created and provides the water to keep it alive. The earth in return provides food for people and animals.

Just as He cares for the earth and its life, He cares for us. Nothing can bring you to life spiritually like the refreshing rain of the Holy Spirit. During those times when you feel dry, burned out, and dying, God can send a shower of His Spirit to revive you and give you new life. Where you felt as though you couldn't go any farther, you experience energy to keep going. Where you felt dry and parched before, you suddenly feel like you've had a drink from the fountain of life. Like the resurrection plant, you begin to unfold from your dehydrated state and open up to breathe again.

Prayer: God, send the rain of the Holy Spirit into my life today. Refresh, revive, and restore me. I want more than a sprinkle. Drench me in Your Spirit. Amen.

Fire and Water

Today's Reading: Psalm 66

"For you, God, tested us; you refined us like silver. You brought us into prison and laid burdens on our backs. You let people ride over our heads; we went through fire and water, but you brought us to a place of abundance" Psalm 66:10-12.

From 1955 until 2003 a popular TV show called "This Is Your Life" aired for forty-three seasons. Each episode featured a special guest who is given a surprise visit or story by people who impacted them throughout their life. Reading this psalm, I was reminded of that show and how much people affect us and our decisions sometimes without us even realizing it until we're older.

The psalmist wrote this song of praise to God as He recalled the mighty acts of God he had witnessed in his lifetime. The intervention of God in his life and the lives of those around him made quite an impact on him. He begins by saying "Shout for joy to God, all the earth! Sing the glory of his name; make his praise glorious. Say to God, How awesome are your deeds! So great is your power that your enemies cringe before you."

He goes on to talk of how God turned the sea into dry land, preserved their lives, and kept their feet from slipping. I too have been amazed when I look back over my life and think about how many times God has rescued me and kept me safe when I didn't even realize it.

"…we went through fire and water, but you brought us to a place of abundance."

Fire and water, two very powerful elements that God's people endured. They didn't just observe them or hear about them, they went through them, and yet they came out victorious on the other side.

Prayer: God, You are worthy to be praised for Your awesome works of power. Thank You for the many times You have brought me through fiery trials to a place of victory and abundance. Amen.

Deliverance from Water

Today's Reading: Psalm 69:1-18

"Save me, O God, for the waters have come up to my neck. I sink in the miry depths, where there is no foothold. I have come into the deep waters; the floods engulf me. I am worn out calling for help; my throat is parched. My eyes fail, looking for my God" Psalm 69:1-3.

Years ago, as a young married woman I experienced depression. I prayed daily for a solution. Others prayed with me. I felt exhausted by the situation. It seemed that I, like the writer, was worn out calling for help. Like the Psalmist, I felt as though I was up to my neck in water and sinking in the mire. Things felt pretty hopeless.

When we're in these situations, it's hard to

keep our head above water. It's a desperate, and sometimes frightening state to be in. It's hard to focus on the good things around us. All we can see is gloom and doom. Even though we may feel as though God isn't listening and our throat is parched from calling for His help, He hasn't abandoned us.

Looking back on that time in my life, I know I could not have made it without God's help. Even though I couldn't see a solution, He was there all the time, holding my head above the water, working all things out for my good. I survived. We all do when we depend on God. It's only when we depend on ourselves or other people that we sometimes find our feet slipping off the edge into the mire below.

An old cliché says, "When you get to the end of your rope tie a knot in it and hang on." But better than that, Romans 8:28 says, "And we know that in all things God works for the good of those who love him, who have been called according to his purpose." If we depend on God, He's faithful to hear our call and act. Hold on to that promise that He's working on your behalf even when the water is up to your neck.

Prayer: God, help me to remember Your promises and cling to them even when it seems all is lost. Thank You for being faithful to me in good times and bad. Amen.

Led Through the Water

Today's Reading: Psalm 77:13-20

"Your path led through the sea, your way
through the mighty waters, though your
footprints were not seen. You led your
people like a flock by the hand of Moses and
Aaron."

A series of large footprints have been
embedded along a busy sidewalk in
downtown Hattiesburg, Mississippi.
They are roughly fourteen inches long. Legend
has it that because of the size of his feet, the
owner, John Wesley Fairley, could never find
shoes that fit him right. There are stories of him
walking barefoot into the federal land office in

Jackson and buying tracts of land.[6] Mr. Fairley left footprints for everyone to see where he had walked.

The psalmist writes that God led His people without leaving any footprints. His hand was on them, guiding them through life, but the human eye couldn't see where He stepped, only the result of His work. We may feel at times as though we're walking blindly through a situation. We don't know which direction to take, but we keep moving, leaving our own set of prints even though we may be going in the wrong direction. But if we rely on God, He will lead us. We may not be able to see His footprints, because sometimes He's leading through water, but His Spirit will lead us down the right path.

Prayer: God, thank You for leading me through the watery trials of my life. Even though I couldn't see Your footprints, I knew You were present. Amen.

---

[6] https://countryroadsmagazine.com/art-and-culture/history/the-mystery-of-hattiesburg-s-footprints-solved/

God: Mightier Than Water

Today's Reading: Psalm 93

"The seas have lifted up, LORD, the seas have lifted up their voice; the seas have lifted up their pounding waves. Mightier than the thunder of the great waters, mightier than the breakers of the sea—the LORD on high is mighty" Psalm 93:3-4.

In Genesis 1, God created the world, giving water and land their boundaries. He spoke the word and put them in place. He has used water to judge sin, defeat enemies, and heal disease. Water in all its forms is powerful and can be dangerous. How many times have we heard a news anchor, meteorologist, or first responder tell us to "turn around, don't drown." It only takes six inches of flood water to knock you off your feet or twelve inches to sweep a car off the road. We might think we can brace ourselves and keep from being swept away, but water is powerful. Too many people have learned this the hard way. Water can move buildings off their foundations, uproot trees, and change the landscape of the earth. But in all its power and glory, it is subject to the Creator.

The Psalmist writes that God is mightier than the thunder of the great waters and the breakers of the sea. He speaks, and the water is subject to Him. "The voice of the LORD is over the waters; the God of glory thunders, the LORD thunders over the mighty waters" Psalm 29:3. God is in control. He has authority over the seas. "He gathers the waters of the sea into jars he puts the deep into storehouses" Psalm 33:7.

Whatever you're facing today, remember that God is mightier than all the forces on earth. Nothing can deter Him from His care for you. The enemy may hinder, but God, the creator of land and sea, has the last word.

"He set the earth on its foundations; it can never be moved. You covered it with the watery depths as with a garment; the waters stood above the mountains. But at your rebuke the waters fled, at the sound of your thunder they took to flight; they flowed over the mountains, they went down into the valleys, to the place you assigned for them" Psalm 104:5-8.

What a mighty God we serve.

Prayer: God, I know that You have all

power and authority over Your creation. Give me the courage to put my life in Your hands completely. Amen.

Water as The Enemy

Today's Reading: Psalm 124

"If the LORD had not been on our side when people attacked us, . . . the raging waters would have swept us away" Psalm 124:1, 5.

On August 24, 1814, British troops led by Rear Admiral Sir George Cockburn marched on Washington, D.C. and set fire to most of the city. With much of the city in flames the next day, British soldiers kept moving through, lighting more fires. They didn't notice the sky turning dark or the thunder and lightning. A tornado formed in the center of the city and headed straight for the British on Capitol Hill. The twister ripped buildings from their foundations and trees up by the roots. British cannons were tossed around by the winds. Several British troops were killed by falling structures and flying debris. The rain continued for two hours, dousing the flames. The British decided it was time to leave. As they were preparing to leave, a conversation was noted between the British Admiral and a Washington resident regarding the storm: The admiral exclaimed, "Madam! Is this the kind of storm to which you are accustomed in this infernal country?" The lady answered, "No, Sir, this is a special interposition of Providence to drive our enemies from our city."[7]

Psalm 124 is a praise for the deliverance God had brought to His people Israel when they faced a formidable enemy. The water mentioned in Psalm 124 is portrayed as the enemy threatening to overwhelm them. God's people had been in trouble more than once, but God was faithful to deliver them over and over. They realized that if the Lord hadn't been on their side, the raging waters would have swept them away.

If you're facing raging waters and you feel as though a flood is about to engulf you, remember that your help "is in the name of the LORD, the Maker of heaven and earth" (v. 8). Like the woman in Washington, D.C. you too can proclaim that there has been divine intervention from God.

---

[7] Fire and Rain: The Storm That Changed D.C. History | Boundary Stones (weta.org)

Prayer: Lord, I know my help comes from You. I trust You to be on my side and rescue me from the raging water I'm facing. Hold back the torrent of flood waters that threaten me. Amen.

Vickie Phelps

Living Water

Water gives life to all of us if we drink it, but we must pick up the glass or cup and drink the contents to benefit from it. Our bodies benefit greatly from the consumption of water. The same is true of living water. We must become acquainted with the giver of living water and accept His gift of life drinking deeply of Him. The water He gives never goes stagnant. It's always moving, alive, sustaining life. In His own words he tells us, "But whoever drinks the water I give them will never thirst." (John 4:14).

Forsaken Waters

Today's Reading Jeremiah 2

"My people have committed two sins: They have forsaken me, the spring of living water, and have dug their own cisterns, broken cisterns that cannot hold water" Jeremiah 2:13.

The home where I grew up as a teenager was an older house. You could call it historical today based on age. Our family no longer owns it, no one lives there, and it is in a state of decay. But when my parents bought the property, an old cistern still stood inside a screened-in area. Evidently the original owners of the house used it for water, but by the time we moved in, it no longer worked. So, we had a broken cistern that didn't hold water and was of no benefit to our family.

Cisterns in ancient agricultural society were dug to store grain and food, and rainwater. Stored rainwater was used especially during the dry season (May through September). But cisterns could suffer cracks in the lining; therefore, water would seep out and a precious source of life was lost.

God said His people had committed two sins. They had forsaken Him, their source of living water, and had dug cisterns looking for their own water supply. In other words, Israel had turned their back on the one true God to go after false gods. But those other gods were like broken cisterns. They couldn't hold water or give life to the people. Only God could do that. He was their spring of living water. They had chosen to dig their own cisterns, and they didn't hold water.

Charles Spurgeon had the following to say about digging our own cisterns. *"When we choose to dig our own cisterns by following our desires over what God wants for us, we are going to lose our life source. Men are in a restless pursuit after satisfaction and earthly things. They have no forethought for their eternal state, the present hour absorbs them. They turn to another and another of earth's broken cisterns, hoping to find water, where not a drop was ever discovered yet."*[8]

---

[8] *The Treasury of David*, Charles Haddon Spurgeon ©1997, Thomas Nelson, Inc.

How can we survive without the living spring that comes from God? We're going to find ourselves in a dehydrated spiritual state because our broken cistern won't hold water. There are too many cracks that allow God's Spirit to leak out. All too soon, we have a dry, empty cistern that doesn't supply us with the life-giving water we need and we're starving spiritually—a thirst that can't be quenched by our own efforts. We need to get our water source from God.

Prayer: God forgive me for trying to dig my own cistern. Help me to seek after the living spring that comes from You. Amen.

Vickie Phelps

Ezekiel: Step into the Water

Today's Reading: Ezekiel 47:1-12

"He measured off another thousand, but now it was a river that I could not cross, because the water had risen and was deep enough to swim in—a river that no one could cross." Ezekiel 47:5.

As a girl, I waded in mudholes after it rained. The water felt good on my feet, but there was mud at the bottom and sometimes you ended up with mud on your feet. My husband and I have vacationed in places where there were streams and rivers clear enough to see the bottom in shallow places. The ocean is a different story. I'm okay with wading in the ocean, but I'm a mediocre swimmer, so I'm not going to get too far out in that big body of water. It's too deep to wade in once you get very far out. You can easily get in over your head.

In a vision, Ezekiel was led by a man to the entrance of the temple in Jerusalem where he saw water coming out from under the threshold of the temple toward the east and from the south side. The man had a measuring line, and he began measuring the water. The water was only ankle deep at this point, but the man kept measuring and led Ezekiel into knee high water, then waist deep water. When he measured again, Ezekiel said, "It was a river that I could not cross, because the water had risen and was deep enough to swim in—a river that no one could cross." (v.5).

Which depth of spiritual water are you in today? Are you wading just deep enough to get your feet wet, attempting to live a Christian life, but not willing to get in too deep? Are you content with just enough water to splash around in? Or maybe you're up to your knees in your Christian experience, but you don't want to get any wetter. You're more in control that way. Waist deep is getting you in where you have to tread water. You're seeking for more of God, but you haven't given in to getting your head wet. That means total commitment.

Water to swim in is ahead of you. All you have to do is take that leap, make the decision to go all out and get soaked from head to foot. This is where you give up your desires and put your full trust in God, allowing Him to be your lifeguard from now on. It's actually a place of freedom because you no longer have to worry if you're getting in too deep. You're already there.

Prayer: God, give me the courage to get into water deep enough for swimming. Make me bold enough to dive into water that will bring me into a soaking wet experience of the Holy Spirit and a closer relationship with You. Amen.

Into Deep Water

Today's Reading: Luke 5:1-11

"When he had finished speaking, he said to Simon, "Put out into deep water, and let down the nets for a catch." Luke 5:4

A crowd had gathered at Lake Gennesaret to hear Jesus teach. The group was crowding around Jesus, so He climbed into Simon's boat and taught the crowd from there. When He finished teaching, He told Simon to launch into deep water and let down his nets.

Simon had tried fishing earlier and didn't catch anything and he was a fisherman by profession, but because Jesus asked him to do it, he obeyed. The nets filled with fish, so many in fact that they had to call their fishing partners to bring their boat over to help. The catch was so big that it filled both boats, and they began to sink.

What if Simon had refused to let down his nets? He was busy cleaning the nets from the day's work. Why try again? What if he had argued with Jesus, as we humans are prone to do, and said, "What's the use?" or maybe, "I've already tried that; it didn't work." We often have our minds made up what we're going to do in a situation and how we're going to do it. We're so determined to do it our way that we take offense if someone comes along and suggests something other than our plan. We are not interested in launching out into deep water. We are happy where we are. The only problem with that thinking is that we miss out on the blessings of a deeper launch. Peter's obedience gave him the biggest catch of his life.

Prayer: Jesus, help me to launch out into the deep water where you have a blessing waiting for me. Amen.

Jesus: Water in His Name

Today's Reading: Mark 9:30-41

"Truly I tell you, anyone who gives you a cup of water in my name because you belong to the Messiah will certainly not lose their reward" Mark 9:41.

Ever watched children play King of the Mountain? Maybe you played it yourself as a child. One child stood on a hill, table, porch, something higher than the others and proclaimed himself king. He was the greatest. Everyone else tried to pull him off his elevated spot. If someone succeeded, they became the king. But they had to watch because now everyone wanted to pull them down.

The disciples had an argument as to who was the greatest among them. Who should be at the top? In our language today, who should be king of the mountain? When Jesus asked what they were arguing about, they wouldn't own up to what they had been saying. He knew of course what they had been discussing. He said, "Anyone who wants to be first must be the very last, and the servant of all." They needed to be willing to be a nobody before they could become somebody for Christ.

From there the discussion moved into who should be allowed to do things in the name of Jesus. Once again, they were concerned about status. John said they had seen someone casting out demons in Jesus' name, but they told him to stop because he wasn't one of them. The status situation again. But Jesus said, "Whoever is not against us is for us." He went on to tell them that anyone who gave them a cup of water in His name because they were one of His would not lose their reward. A simple thing like a cup of water given in the name of Christ would be accepted.

Sometimes the status situation gets out of hand, among people, denominations, families, and Christians. Jesus welcomed all who came to Him. He didn't judge people by their social standing. Anyone who gave or did something in His name because of Him would be giving an acceptable gift.

Prayer: Jesus, remove any pride or prejudice in my heart. Give me a heart to receive what is given me in Your name. Fill me with gratitude for the giver as well as the gift. Amen.

Jesus Commands the Water

Today's Reading: Luke 8:22-25

"He got up and rebuked the wind and the raging waters; the storm subsided, and all was calm. "Where is your faith?" he asked his disciples. In fear and amazement, they asked one another, "Who is this? He commands even the winds and the water, and they obey him" Luke 8:24-25.

My husband and I stood at the door and watched golf ball sized hail rain down on our house and yard. A few of the stones were even larger. We knew it was doing damage to the roof of our house and other things as well, but we had no control over it. All we could do was watch and wait for the storm to pass.

Jesus and His disciples climbed into a boat one day to cross the lake. Jesus lay down in the bottom of the boat and went to sleep. Meanwhile, a storm arose. It was so fierce that the boat began filling with water. The frightened disciples woke Jesus. "We're going to drown." Jesus stood and rebuked the winds and the waves and calm settled over the sea.

Jesus said to the disciples, "Where is your faith?"

But the disciples looked at one another and said, "What kind of man is this that can command wind and water and they obey Him?"

They had been traveling with Jesus for some time and witnessed His miracles, but they still didn't know His complete power. He had authority over even the elements. They had never seen anyone like Him before.

The physical and the spiritual storms that come into our lives threaten to sink our ship sometimes. We may not know which direction to take, but we know someone with the authority to calm the storm and He has also given us authority to use His name to overcome what confronts us. When we pray, He will exercise His authority through us. Ole Hallesby, the noted theologian and writer from Norway said, "Prayer is the risen Jesus coming in with His resurrection power, given free rein in our lives, and then using His authority to enter any situation and change things." [9]

---

[9] https://www.azquotes.com/quote/545459

Jesus will use His authority to calm the storm that is threatening us if we give Him free rein in our lives and trust Him.

Prayer: Jesus, take free rein in my life today and calm the storm raging around me. Use Your authority to work out the circumstances I am helpless to change. Amen.

Vickie Phelps

Jesus Changes Water

Today's Reading: John 2:1-10, NLT.

"But his mother told the servants, "Do whatever he tells you" John 2:5, NLT.

The servants in the reading today discovered they were out of wine in the middle of a wedding celebration. We don't know their exact reactions, but they didn't know what to do about the situation. Maybe they were wringing their hands, afraid to tell the bridegroom he was out of wine. But Jesus' mother found out about it, and she told Him. He didn't really give her any encouragement about the situation, but she told the servants to do whatever he said to do.

How many times have you uttered the words, "It's impossible"? How often have you found yourself in a situation that seemed hopeless, with no solution in sight? When my husband who has health issues wanted to retire from his job, I said, "there's no way." I wasn't against him retiring to take it easier. I just didn't see how we could do it financially. Over the next few months, I saw God work on our behalf in a way that made it possible for him to retire and still have a good income. In my thinking, it seemed impossible, but God had a plan in mind.

Jesus can change the water of our lives but first we must be like the servants in the story today and do as He ask even if it looks silly or impossible. Those servants may have had thoughts like: "That's the craziest thing I've ever heard," "You can't make wine from water," "We can't serve water to the guests, it will get us into trouble." Sound familiar? Sometimes we may feel like Jesus is asking us to do something that does not make a lot of sense. We are thinking: "I'm going to look pretty silly doing this, and people are going to laugh at me." In other words, we're not thinking about Him and what He can do, but we're worried about how we're going to appear by getting involved.

We may not know what they were thinking, but the one thing we do know about the servants is they obeyed Jesus' command. The result: A supernatural miracle occurred. The water was changed into wine, the best tasting wine at the wedding. When the situation looks impossible, we need to remember that we serve a God of supernatural power. Sometimes we just need to push our thoughts and pride aside and obey His command and watch while He turns the water of our lives into the best tasting results possible.

Prayer: Jesus, help me recognize that all things are possible with You and to set aside my doubt and pride and embrace Your power to work a miracle in my situation. Strengthen my faith to be an obedient servant no matter how impractical or strange Your request may sound to me and those around me. Amen.

Born of Water

Today's Reading: John 3:1-21

"Jesus answered, "Very truly I tell you, no one can enter the kingdom of God unless they are born of water and the Spirit. Flesh gives birth to flesh, but the Spirit gives birth to spirit" John 3:5-6.

Conception and the birth of a new life is truly a miracle designed by God. As the oldest of five children, I remember when my two youngest siblings were born, especially the last one. Suddenly there was a new person in our family, a child born of water, a physical birth, one who became part of my responsibility as the oldest child. I watched him grow out of baby clothes and into regular children's clothes. I read books to him and babysat him when our parents went shopping. But one day, it came time for me to leave home, and from that point on, I saw very little of my siblings. Today, when I see them, they're all mature adults with children and grandchildren of their own, and they are strong Christians who matured spiritually as well as physically.

Nicodemus stepped out into the night to go see the man called Jesus. As a member of the Jewish ruling council, it might not be looked on with favor to be seen with Him but under the cover of darkness, He slipped out to see this man who taught with authority and worked miracles. He wanted to know more about Him.

He spoke to Jesus. "Rabbi, we know that you are a teacher who has come from God. For no one could perform the signs you are doing if God were not with him."

Jesus' reply surprised him. "No one can see the kingdom of God unless they are born again."

Nicodemus thought He was speaking of a physical birth, but Jesus explained that man is born naturally of the flesh, but He must also experience a spiritual birth. Without that spiritual birth, we cannot enter the kingdom of God. Just as our mother's gave birth to us, bringing us into the world and making us a part of our earthly family, we must also be born into the family of God. We must experience a spiritual birth. Our parents raised us to adulthood, teaching and training us how to live in the world. We must also grow from a newborn Christian into a mature follower of God. It doesn't happen overnight. It's a daily process of walking with God, spending time with Him, and following His plan for our lives.

Prayer: Jesus, draw me into an intimate, closer relationship with You. Help me to live by Your truths and share that light with others. Amen.

Well of Living Water

Today's Reading: John 4:1-26

"Jesus answered her, "If you knew the gift of God and who it is that asks you for a drink, you would have asked him, and he would have given you living water" John 4:10.

Have you ever wanted something so badly you would do whatever it took to obtain it, even if it meant working two jobs or doing without something else you needed or wanted? But once you got it, it didn't make you happy. You weren't the contented, excited person you dreamed you would be if you had the object. It didn't change your life for the better. It's kind of like children at Christmas. They can't wait to open presents, and they fly through the wrapping paper one after the other until they have all been opened. Days later, the gifts may lie on the floor abandoned for something else that caught their attention.

When Jesus sat down at Jacob's well in Sychar, a woman came out to draw water, and He asked her for a drink. Surprised, she asked Him why a Jew would ask a Samaritan for a drink since Jews did not associate with Samaritans. Jesus replied that He could give her living water if she asked and she would never thirst again.

"Jesus answered, "Everyone who drinks this water will be thirsty again, but whoever drinks the water I give them will never thirst. Indeed, the water I give them will become in them a spring of water welling up to eternal life" John 4:13-14.

Never mind that He was a Jew and she a Samaritan, living water was available for her.

We're sometimes guilty of thirsting for things that won't satisfy us. The object of our thirst looks good, other people seem to be enjoying it, and it got good reviews on Amazon so it must be wonderful. But like a child at Christmas, weeks later, maybe even days later, we've abandoned the object because it didn't live up to our expectations, and we're still thirsty. The problem lies with what we're thirsty for. We need to abandon the search in the world for something to quench our thirst and ask Jesus to give us a drink of the living water He offers. He promised we will never thirst again.

Prayer: Jesus, help me to lose my thirst for the world and all its trinkets and pleasures. Give me a thirst for living water from You. Amen.

Vickie Phelps

Water for my Feet

Today's Reading: John 13:1-17

"After that, he poured water into a basin and began to wash his disciples' feet, drying them with the towel that was wrapped around him" John 13:5.

S ome time ago I went to a wedding where the bride and groom washed each other's feet. I had never seen this as a part of the wedding ceremony before, but the love and humility it displayed was very touching. What a wonderful commitment they were making to each other, that they would love and serve one another for ever.

In Bible times foot washing was necessary because folks wore sandals, and they walked to get many places. This meant their feet were covered in dust from the roads. It was customary for a host to offer water for visitors to wash their feet when they entered the house.

Even though washing someone's feet was a duty that servants usually performed Jesus willingly carried out this menial task for His disciples. He poured water into a basin and wrapped a towel around His waist. That act in itself speaks of His selfless humanity. He didn't wait for someone else to pour the water or bring Him a towel. He carried out even these small tasks. He loved the disciples, and He wanted them to understand that they must be willing to serve others as well as being served themselves. "No servant is greater than his master, nor is a messenger greater than the one who sent him" (v. 16).

How willing are we to serve others? In a culture obsessed with "my rights," and "it's all about me," we need to remind ourselves of the example Christ set for us. Washing feet may not appeal to us. We might not want to be that familiar with someone. It might even cause us to turn up our nose, but the lesson that Jesus taught is we're not too good to serve someone else whether its washing their feet or some other act of love.

Prayer: Jesus, help me be willing to serve others no matter how distasteful it may seem. Show me how to follow Your example by laying aside any prideful thoughts or prejudice I may have. Amen.

Planting and Watering

Today's Reading: 1 Corinthians 3:1-23

"I planted the seed, Apollos watered it, but God has been making it grow. So neither the one who plants nor the one who waters is anything, but only God, who makes things grow" 1 Corinthians 3:6-7.

Gardeners take a tiny seed, bury it in the ground and water the soil then wait for the results. That tiny seed sprouts and pushes its way up through soil, sometimes firmly packed soil, until it breaks through to the outside. God created that seed to do this naturally. It almost seems impossible that a tiny sprout or vine can push through packed soil, but God created it to do just that. The gardener can plant and water and tend to the growing plants but only God can make the seed grow into a plant that produces beautiful blooms or delicious produce. The gardener plants and waters, but God brings about the result.

It's the same with working for God. We have a part to play in spreading the gospel, mentoring other Christians, and working in the church. We can do a lot or a little, but the results still lie in God's hands. It will all come to fruition in His time. In fact, we may never see the end result of some of our work. The person we witness to may never come to know Christ until after we are gone, but it's still rewarding and worth the effort. A Greek proverb says it this way: "A society grows great when old men plant trees whose shade they know they shall never sit in." I believe it's true of God's kingdom. It will grow and flourish when we all work together whether we are a part of it at the end or not.

Paul wanted the Corinthian church to know that it didn't matter who planted or watered, both were important, but what did matter is that God gave the final increase, and they needed to look to Him for the results. They might follow one man or the other, but it is God who will bring about life at the end and Him they should keep their eyes on.

Prayer: Lord, help me to do my part in planting and watering whether I see the end results or not. I'll leave the results in Your hands. Amen.

Bitter or Sweet Water

Today's Reading: James 3:1-12

"With the tongue we praise our Lord and
Father, and with it we curse human beings, who
have been made in God's likeness. Out of the
same mouth come praise and cursing. My
brothers and sisters, this should not be. Can
both fresh water and saltwater flow from the
same spring?" James 3:9-10.

A s a boy, my husband and his dad dug
water wells. It was hard, backbreaking
work, but if the water was good, it was
well worth the labor it took to get it. One of the
wells they dug produced hard water which you
could drink but it didn't work well for other
things. Soap wouldn't lather as well in the hard
water. One thing that never happened though

was getting both good and bad water out of the same well. It was always one or the other.

James mentioned this same principle in his writings. He asked the question, "Can both fresh water and saltwater flow from the same spring?" He asked this in regard to people using their mouth to praise God on one hand and curse someone else out of the same mouth. He answered his own question by saying, "...this should not be."

This same principle can be applied to our Christian life. Do we act the same all the time or do we play both sides? Just as fresh water and saltwater cannot both come from the same fountain, we cannot live for God and Satan at the same time. We must make a choice to give up the world or give up eternal life. Otherwise, our lives are lived in vain. We must be like the fountain that only produces sweet water and the mouth that only gives praise to God. Only then can we be the example of Christ that others need to see.

Prayer: Lord, help me to choose to live in a way that pleases You and points others to the cross. Let my words be acceptable to You and my life an example of a well full of sweet water that others can drink from. Amen.

Springs of Living Water

Today's Reading: Revelation 7:13-17

"For the Lamb at the center of the throne will
be their shepherd; 'he will lead them to springs
of living water.' 'And God will wipe away
every tear from their eyes'" Revelation 7:17.

Tears streamed down my cheeks as I stood
by the casket of a dear friend. I had lost
someone I leaned on for advice and
wisdom, both spiritual and natural. But even in
my grief I knew he was in a better place. I would
miss his kind spirit and Christian leadership, but
I would see him again someday.

One of the good things about being a
Christian is the knowledge that we have a future
home in heaven where there will be no pain,
hunger, thirst, death, or shedding of tears.

Revelation tells us that God will wipe away every tear. And the Lamb, Jesus Christ, will lead us to springs of living water. Water to drink that gives us eternal life and takes away the sting of death.

In the story of the woman at the well of Sychar in John chapter four, Jesus spoke to her of living water. "Jesus answered, "Indeed, the water I give them will become in them a spring of water welling up to eternal life." (v.14). The springs of living water that He shared with her will be a reality in heaven as the Good Shepherd leads us to them. She received that spring the day she met Jesus, and it will come in all its fullness when we reach our heavenly destination.

Prayer: Jesus, let me drink of the springs of living water that I may obtain the eternal life that comes from You. Amen

Water of Life

Today's Reading: Revelation 21:1-27

"To the thirsty I will give water without cost
from the spring of the water of life. Those who
are victorious will inherit all this, and I will be
their God and they will be my children"
Revelation 21:6-7.

I f you've ever watched very many western
movies, a lot of them contained scenes of
people fighting over water rights. One
rancher dams up the stream and shuts off the
supply to a neighbor who then threatens him if
he doesn't let him have water. Sometimes it
affects entire towns. We know these are only
movies, but one thing is for sure. Water is a
precious commodity.

Every month we pay a bill for water that

we've used. Some months it's more than others, especially in the summer months when we water our lawn and garden. Since water is a necessity, we can't just decide not to pay. If we do that, the water company will shut off access to water at our house.

Someday, we will no longer need to pay for or fight for water. John wrote in the Book of Revelations that Jesus will give us water without cost from a spring of the water of life.

One of the great benefits of living for God is access to all that He has, not only here on earth but also in heaven. Because we're a part of His family, we are moving to heaven one day where we can drink water that doesn't cost us anything, live in a mansion that's already been paid for, eat fruit from a tree that we didn't plant and spend all the time we want with Him in worship and praise. The victorious will inherit all of this.

Sometimes life here on earth gets tedious and so busy that we don't spend as much time in His presence as we would like to or need to. As we choose to spend time with Him, our relationship with Him grows stronger and more intimate. We may as well prepare ourselves for the move to heaven by spending some quality time with Him, drinking from the spring of the water of life before we ever arrive at our destination.

Prayer: Lord, help me to choose to spend more time with You down here in preparation for being with You in heaven. Let me daily drink of the water of life. Amen.

Bibliography

The Treasury of David: Spurgeon's Great Commentary on Psalms, Spurgeon, Charles Haddon, Updated by Clarke, Roy H., Thomas Nelson, Inc., Nashville, Tennessee, © 1997.

Zondervan Illustrated Bible Backgrounds Commentary on Old Testament, Zondervan Publishing, Grand Rapids, Michigan, © 2002.

Amen and Good Night God: A Book of Evening Prayers, Huddleston, Jo, Tyndale House Publishers, Inc. Wheaton, Illinois, © 1995.

www.ingramcontent.com/pod-product-compliance
Lightning Source LLC
Chambersburg PA
CBHW071147120626
46546CB00006B/2150